My SCHOOL YARD GARDEN

STEVE RICH

D1313541

NSTA Kids

National Science Teachers Association

Arlington, Virginia

National Science Teachers Association

Claire Reinburg, Director
Wendy Rubin, Managing Editor
Andrew Cooke, Senior Editor
Amanda O'Brien, Associate Editor
Amy America, Book Acquisitions Coordinator

ART AND DESIGN
Will Thomas Jr., Director
Joe Butera, Cover, Interior Design

PRINTING AND PRODUCTION
Catherine Lorrain, Director

NATIONAL SCIENCE TEACHERS ASSOCIATION
David L. Evans, Executive Director
David Beacom, Publisher

1840 Wilson Blvd., Arlington, VA 22201
www.nsta.org/store
For customer service inquiries, please call 800-277-5300.

Lexile® measure: AD 1110L

Copyright © 2015 by the National Science Teachers Association.
All rights reserved. Printed in the United States of America.
18 17 16 15   4 3 2 1

NSTA is committed to publishing material that promotes the best in inquiry-based science education. However, conditions of actual use may vary, and the safety procedures and practices described in this book are intended to serve only as a guide. Additional precautionary measures may be required. NSTA and the authors do not warrant or represent that the procedures and practices in this book meet any safety code or standard of federal, state, or local regulations. NSTA and the authors disclaim any liability for personal injury or damage to property arising out of or relating to the use of this book, including any of the recommendations, instructions, or materials contained therein.

PERMISSIONS

Book purchasers may photocopy, print, or e-mail up to five copies of an NSTA book chapter for personal use only; this does not include display or promotional use. Elementary, middle, and high school teachers may reproduce forms, sample documents, and single NSTA book chapters needed for classroom or noncommercial, professional-development use only. E-book buyers may download files to multiple personal devices but are prohibited from posting the files to third-party servers or websites, or from passing files to non-buyers. For additional permission to photocopy or use material electronically from this NSTA Press book, please contact the Copyright Clearance Center (CCC) (*www.copyright.com*; 978-750-8400). Please access *www.nsta.org/permissions* for further information about NSTA's rights and permissions policies.

Library of Congress Cataloging-in-Publication Data
Rich, Steve, 1962-
  My school yard garden / by Steve Rich.
    pages cm
  Audience: K to Grade 3.
  ISBN 978-1-938946-21-9 (pbk.) -- ISBN 978-1-941316-94-8 (e-book) 1. School gardens--Juvenile literature. I. Title.
  SB55.R53 2014
  635--dc23
                        2014033834

Cataloging-in-Publication Data are also available from the Library of Congress for the e-book.
e-LCCN: 2014035484

DEDICATED TO THE MEMORY OF MY FATHER,

Rochell Rich, Jr.,

FOR MAKING OUR GARDEN AND EVERY OUTDOOR SPACE
A PLACE FOR ME TO LEARN AND GROW.

There's a garden in my school yard that is here to help us learn about growing plants and how the plants help animals find what they need to survive.

Some of the animals that stop in the garden are on a long migration from one place to another, while other animals live near the school year-round.

When large buildings such as schools take the place of natural spaces such as woods or fields, it is important for people to provide the resources that have been taken away. In the school yard garden, I have learned to grow seedlings that provide food for insects and birds.

Host plants such as dill or milkweed are food for caterpillars, and plants with berries are food for birds.

Scraps and cuttings from the plants go into a compost bin so they can decompose and become fertilizer.

Sometimes we add banana peels and apple cores from the cafeteria.

8

As the plant scraps rot, they produce heat that we measure with a thermometer.

Worms come to the bin to eat rotting leaves. The worms might in turn become meals for birds.

Along with the plants and compost bin in the garden is a patio made of concrete blocks. We can use the space to make a graph or write science words with chalk.

The words we write in chalk list what the plants need—sunshine, air, soil, and water—and what the animals need—air, shelter, a water source, and food.

In the garden, a pile of tree limbs makes a nice shelter for lizards and other small animals, while the birdhouse we made is a shelter that keeps young birds safe and warm.

For water in the garden, there is a birdbath where the birds splash around and drink and a puddle area for butterflies to take in moisture and minerals from sandy soil.

On benches nearby, we can sit quietly to write in our nature journals. We record our school yard observations of animals that visit the garden.

We also make sketches to go with what we write, like the one I made of a bird pulling a worm from the compost pile.

After drawing the bird
with the worm, I began
to think about how the
two animals would fit
into a food chain.

I sketched it out: The Sun gives light and warmth to plants,
the worm eats leaves, and the bird eats the worm.

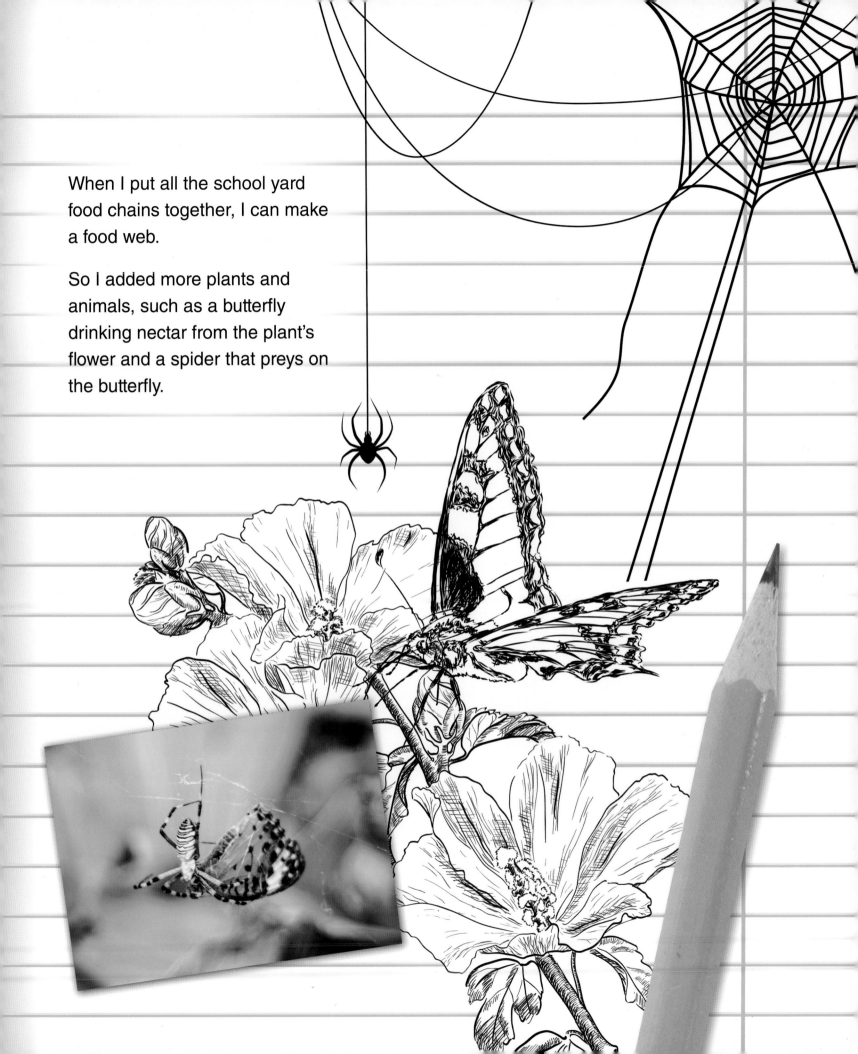

When I put all the school yard food chains together, I can make a food web.

So I added more plants and animals, such as a butterfly drinking nectar from the plant's flower and a spider that preys on the butterfly.

In a plot in the garden, we grow vegetables and herbs that people can eat, so that means humans can also be part of a food chain.

We give some of the vegetables to the local shelter for homeless people. My teacher says gardens have been used to help people for a very long time.

We even planted a history garden using ideas from America's past. First, we planted a Native American garden using plants called the three sisters.

THREE SISTERS

Beans, squash, and corn can grow together in the tradition of the Iroquois people. The bean vine grows up the cornstalk, and the squash plant prevents weeds from growing around its roots.

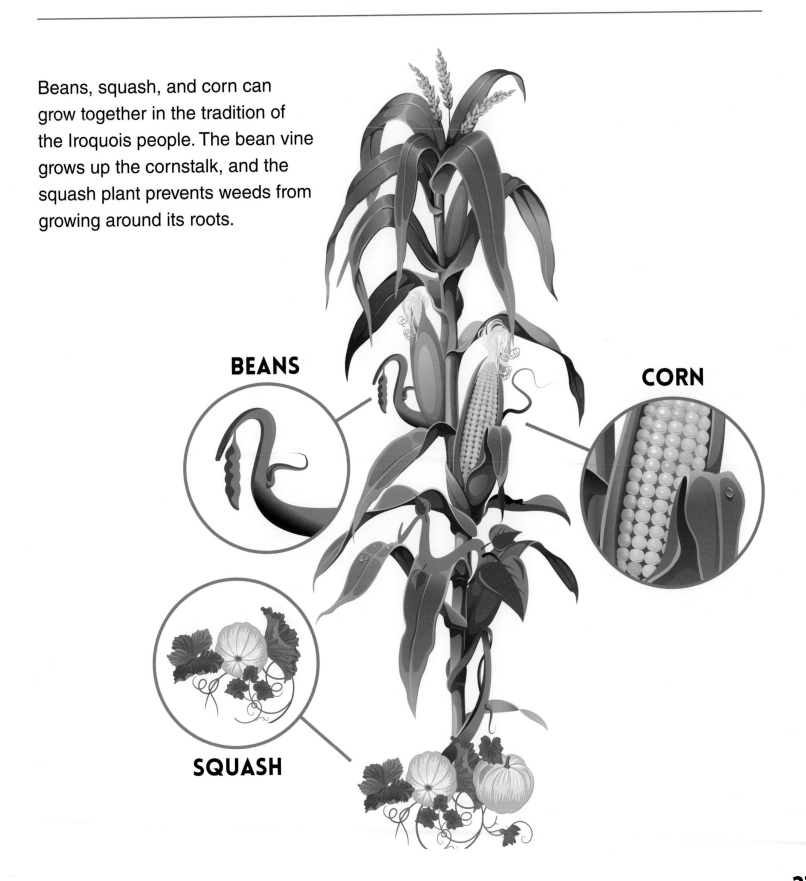

BEANS

CORN

SQUASH

The history garden also has a place for herbs used by American colonists. We planted parsley, oregano, sage, and lemon balm.

In colonial times, herbs were sometimes used the way we would use medicine today. At other times, herbs were used in colorful dyes for clothing or as flavoring for food.

I wanted to know how plants survive when people and animals eat so many. I learned that the animals give the plants just as much as they take from them.

A seed forms after a plant is pollinated with pollen from another flower, but the pollen first must be carried to the plant. Often, a bee, butterfly, hummingbird, or bat carries the pollen.

For plants to survive, their seeds must be scattered to new places where the plants have enough room to grow. One way this happens is when a seed sticks to a bird's feather for a time and then falls off in another location.

Seeds can also end up in places to grow when a bird buries the seeds it collected, planning to come back and eat them later. Another way they grow in new places is when an animal eats fruit and drops the waste (including undigested seeds) someplace where the seeds have plenty of room to grow.

Just as the garden provides animals and plants more space to grow, it also gives us more room to learn.

I like to think of it this way: The seeds I plant in the school garden are like ideas. I plant them, and the teacher helps me figure out what they need to grow.

Glossary

COMPOST BIN

a large container where scraps of plants can be kept while they decompose

FOOD CHAIN

the group of animals and plants that recycle the Sun's energy (for example, a parsley plant, a caterpillar, a bird, and a bobcat)

FOOD WEB

two or more food chains with common elements

HABITAT

the place in which an animal or plant lives

MIGRATE (MIGRATION)

to move from one place to another over a great distance in response to changes in weather, food sources, or other conditions that affect survival

NATURE JOURNAL

a notebook in which a student or scientist writes about what he or she observes outdoors

NECTAR

the small amount of sweet liquid found at the center of a flower

NUTRIENTS

the parts of the soil that help nourish a plant

POLLEN

the very small, usually yellow, dustlike pieces flowers need to exchange to make seeds; usually moved from one flower to another by insects, birds, bats, or wind

POLLINATOR

any animal that aids in carrying pollen from one flower to another

PREDATOR

an animal that preys on another animal for food

PREY

an animal pursued by another animal, a predator, as a source of food

SHELTER

the place where an animal finds safety, such as in a tree or under a rock

WATER CYCLE

the movement of water through the Earth's surface and atmosphere

Information for Parents and Teachers

Adults are encouraged to use this book as a catalyst for gardening with students at home and at school. If you are the parent of a school-age child, inquire at his or her school if any teachers are involved in or interested in gardening with their students. Here is a list of ways you might be able to help the school:

- Volunteer to be the extra adult that teachers often need when planting in the school yard.

- Donate plants from your yard, such as perennials that can be separated to create new plantings.

- Loan gardening equipment to the school if you cannot afford to donate expensive tools.

- Get training from local extension agents to become a Master Gardener, and share this expertise with the school personnel and students.

- Help students build birdhouses or feeders to attract birds to the school yard.

- Shop for marked-down seeds at the end of the season at local garden centers so you can share them with your child's teacher.

If you are a teacher, talk with your school administrator to ask for permission to garden in the school yard. For teaching ideas and suggestions for building or planting an outdoor classroom, consider some of the lessons in *Outdoor Science: A Practical Guide* or *Bringing Outdoor Science In*, both from NSTA Press, available at *www. nsta.org/store* along with other books related to outdoor learning with students. All teachers of science should carefully consider the ideas in *A Framework for K–12 Science Education* (NRC 2012). Additionally, teachers should consult state science standards and the *Next Generation Science Standards*, which are based in part on the *Framework*.